ROCK & POP

Male Voice Grade 6
VOCALS

ROCK & POP

D041656Z

TRINITY
COLLEGE LONDON

THE EXAM AT A GLANCE

For your Rock & Pop exam you will need to perform a set of **three songs** and one of the **Session skills** assessments, either **Playback** or **Improvising**. You can choose the order in which you play your set-list.

Song 1

Choose a song from this book

OR from www.trinityrock.com

Song 2

Choose a different song from this book

OR from www.trinityrock.com

OR perform a song you have chosen yourself: this could be your own cover version or a song you have written. It should be at the same level as the songs in this book. See the website for detailed requirements.

Song 3: Technical focus

Choose one of the Technical focus songs from this book, which cover three specific technical elements.

Session skills

Choose either **Playback** or **Improvising**.

When you are preparing for your exam please check on **www.trinityrock.com** for the most up-to-date information and requirements as these can change from time to time.

CONTENTS

Trinity College London's Rock & Pop syllabus and supporting publications have been devised and produced in association with Faber Music and Peters Edition London.

Trinity College London
Registered office:
89 Albert Embankment
London SE1 7TP UK
T + 44 (0)20 7820 6100
F + 44 (0)20 7820 6161
E music@trinitycollege.co.uk
www.trinitycollege.co.uk

Registered in the UK. Company no. 02683033
Charity no. 1014792
Patron HRH The Duke of Kent KG

Copyright © 2012 Trinity College London
First published in 2012 by Trinity College London

Cover and book design by Chloë Alexander
Brand development by Andy Ashburner @ Caffeinehit (www.caffeinehit.com)
Photographs courtesy of Rex Features Ltd
Printed in England by Caligraving Ltd

Audio produced, mixed and mastered by Tom Fleming
Backing tracks arranged by Tom Fleming
Musicians
Vocals: Bo Walton, Brendan Reilly, Alison Symons & Hannah Bridge
Piano/keyboards: Dave Maric
Guitar: Tom Fleming
Bass: Ben Hillyard
Drums: George Double
Studio Engineer: Joel Davies www.thelimehouse.com

All rights reserved

ISBN: 978-0-85736-260-5

SONGS CANNONBALL

Damien Rice
Words and Music by Damien Rice

♩ = 74 Gently

with pedal

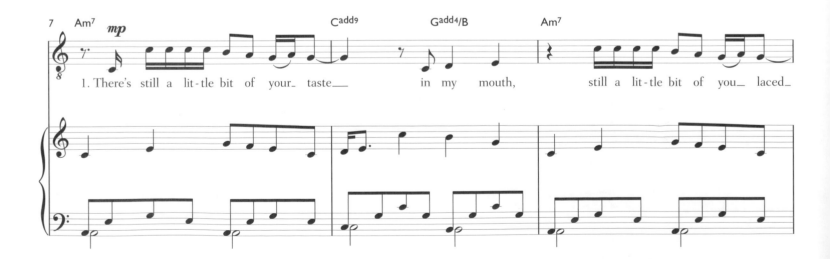

1. There's still a lit-tle bit of your taste in my mouth, still a lit-tle bit of you laced

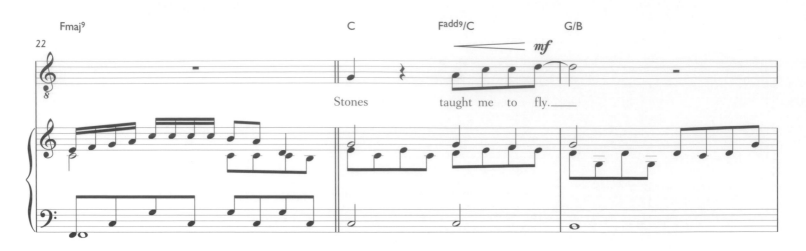

So come on, cou - rage, teach me to be shy;___ 'cause it's not hard_

__ to fall,_ and I don't wan - na scare_ her. It's not hard to fall,__ and I

don't wan - na lose.__ It's not hard to grow when you know that you just___ don't know._

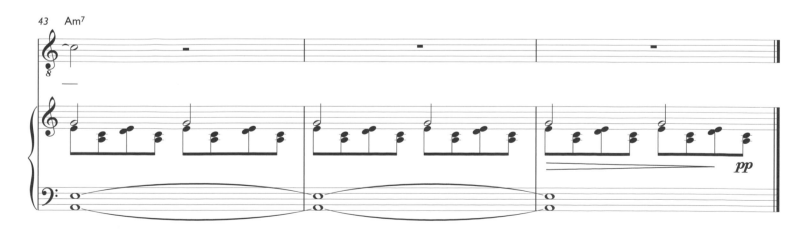

SONGS I CAN SEE CLEARLY NOW

Johnny Nash
Words and Music by Johnny Nash

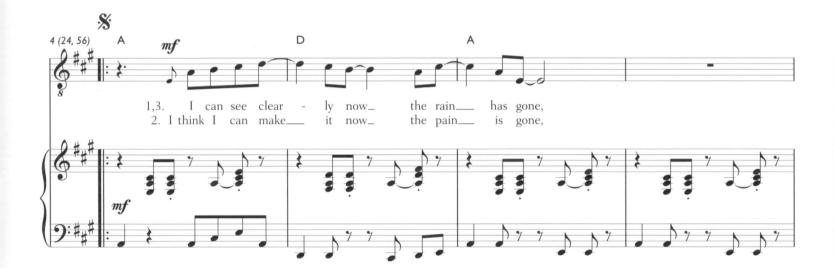

1,3. I can see clear - ly now_ the rain_ has gone,
2. I think I can make_ it now_ the pain_ is gone,

I can see all_ ob - sta - cles in my way._
all of the bad_ feel - ings have dis - ap - peared.

Gone are the dark___ clouds that had___ me blind.
Here is that rain - bow I've___ been pray - ing for.___
It's gon-na be a bright,_

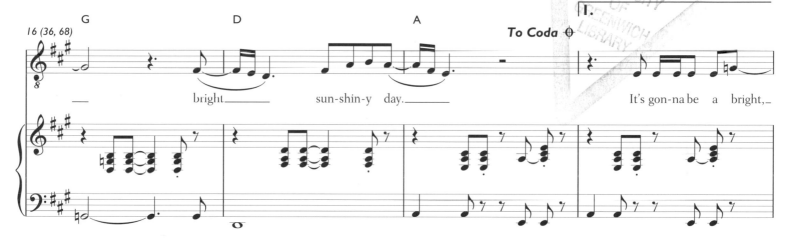

bright___ sun-shin-y day.___ It's gon-na be a bright,_

To Coda ⊕

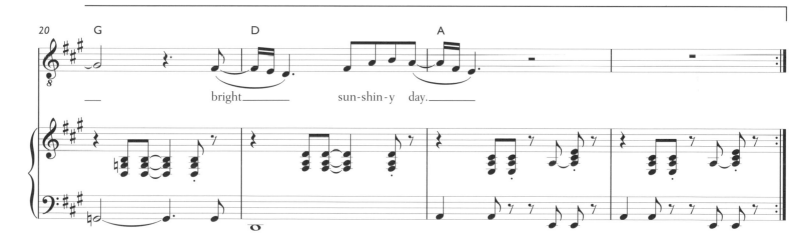

bright___ sun-shin-y day.___

2.

Look all a - round,___ there's no thing but blue skies.___

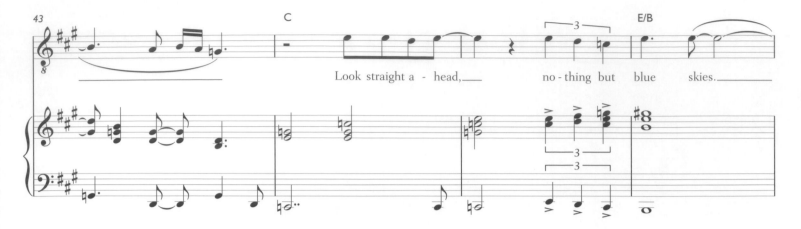

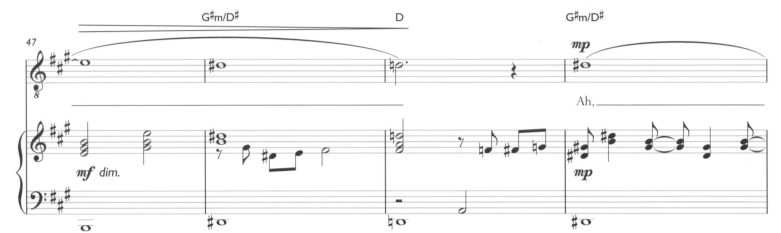

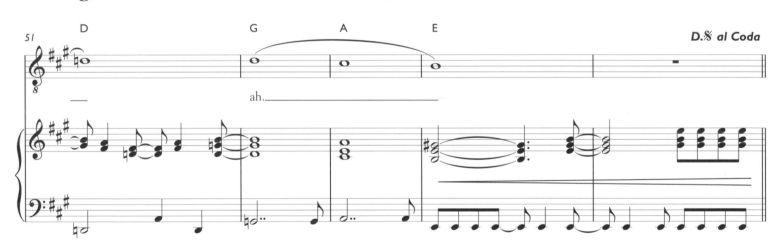

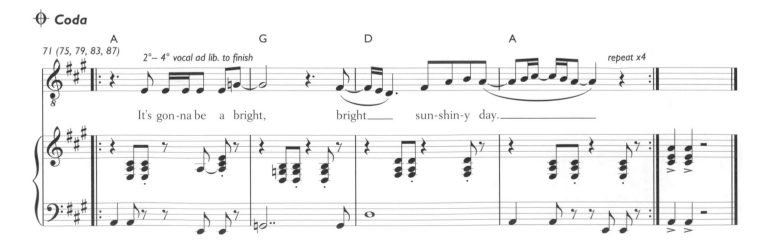

SONGS WILD HORSES

The Rolling Stones
Words and Music by Mick Jagger and Keith Richards

1. Child - hood liv-ing is ea - sy to do.
2. I know I've dreamed you a sin and a

lie,

The things you want - ed,
I have my free - dom

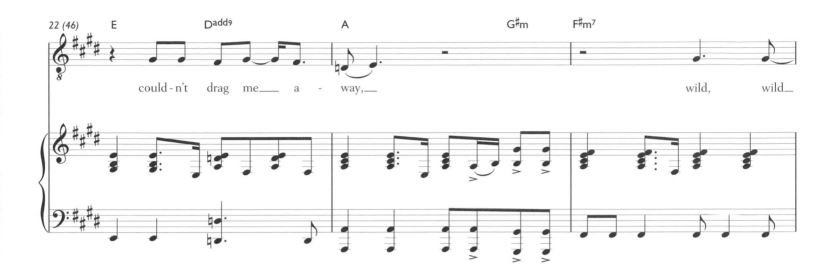

could-n't drag me a - way, wild, wild

1.

hor - ses could-n't drag me a - way.

2.

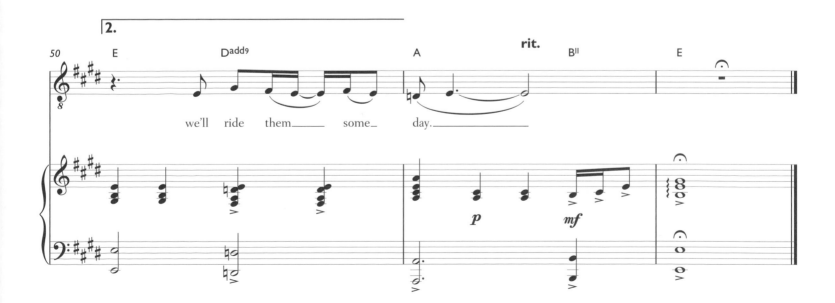

we'll ride them some day.

YOUR PAGE NOTES

SONGS NEUTRON STAR COLLISION

Muse
Words and Music by Matthew Bellamy

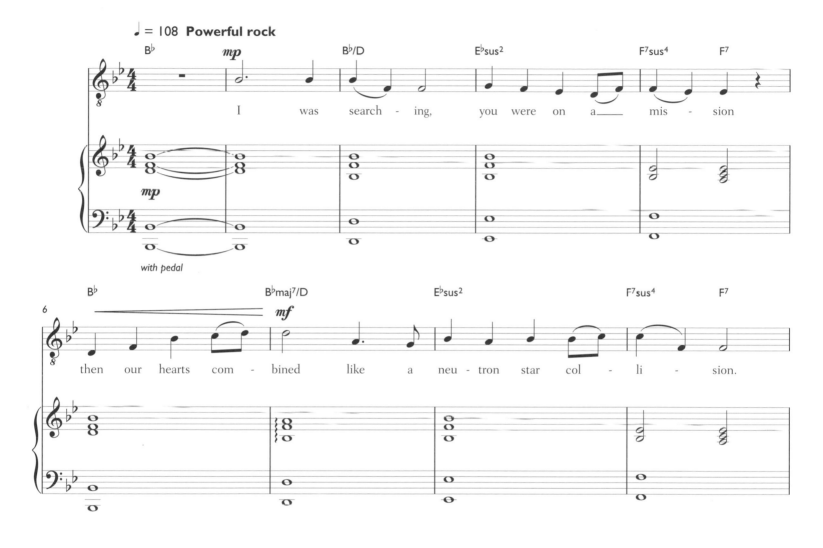

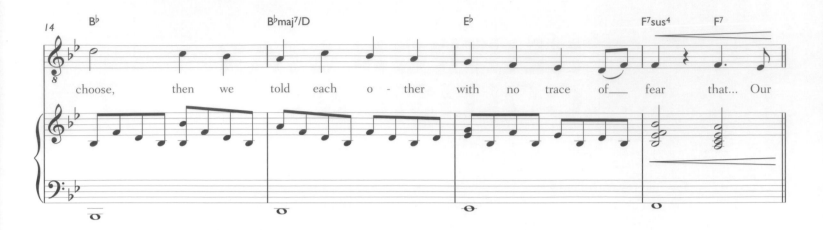

choose, then we told each o - ther with no trace of___ fear that... Our

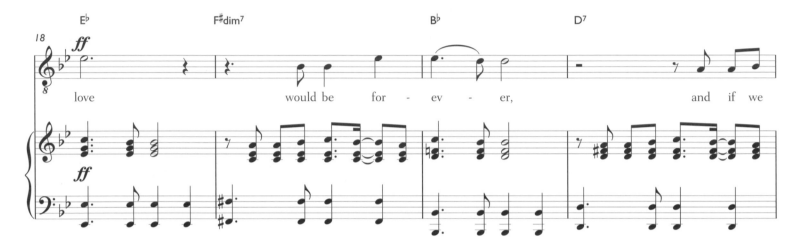

love would be for - ev - er, and if we

die, we die to - ge - ther. And

lie, I said nev - er, be - cause our

love ... would be for - ev - er. The

Faster, with a driving beat (♩ = 128)

world ... is bro - ken, ha - los fail to____

____ glis - ten, you try to make a diff - 'rence but____

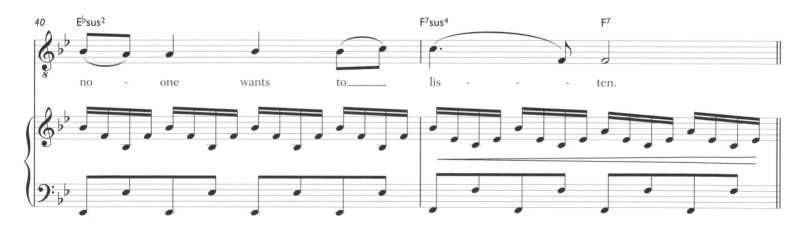

no - one wants to____ lis - - ten.

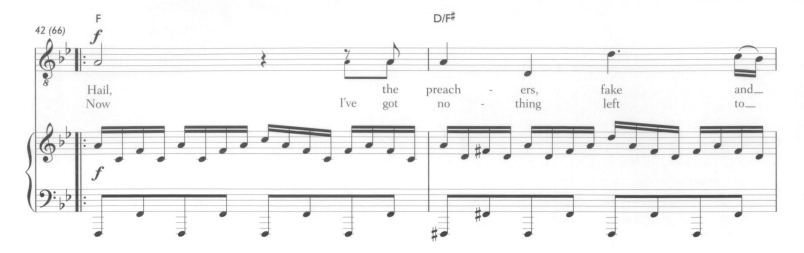

Hail,
Now

the preach - ers, fake and
I've got no - thing left to

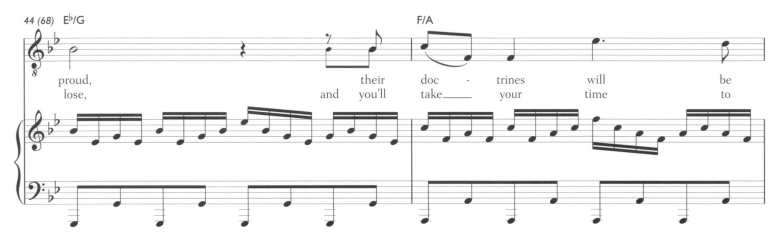

proud, their doc - trines will be
lose, and you'll take___ your time to

cloud, then they'll dis - si - pate like snow - flakes in an___
choose, I can tell you now with - out a trace of

o - cean... But love is for -
fear that... My love will be

-ev - er   and we'll die,

we'll die to - ge - ther.   And lie,

I   say nev - er,   be - cause our love
I   will nev - er,   be - cause our love

could be   for - ev - er.
will be   for - ev - er.

TAINTED LOVE

In your exam, you will be assessed on the following technical elements:

1 Rhythmic control

Although some of the rhythms are quite complex, you should aim to make them sound natural. The lyrics move quite quickly in places, so try speaking these sections first, starting at a slower speed and articulating the consonants clearly. Aim to make your entries confident and precise: count carefully to make sure that you come in at exactly the right place each time.

2 Singing ad lib

From bar 77, you have the opportunity to ad lib and put your personal mark on the song. Practise singing this section in a variety of ways – exploring different melodic, rhythmic and dynamic ideas – and decide what works best, making sure that you follow the chord sequence. Although the improvisation needs to sound spontaneous, it is a good idea to have some riffs worked out in advance.

3 Singing slides

In bars 35, 65 and 72 a straight line has been added between two notes. This indicates that the singer needs to slide between them. Make sure you know your starting and ending pitch – and how soon you need to reach the second pitch. This technique could be included in your vocal warm-ups. You could set yourself different pitches to slide between and vary the duration to develop your control.

TAINTED LOVE

demo   backing

Soft Cell

Words and Music by Ed Cobb

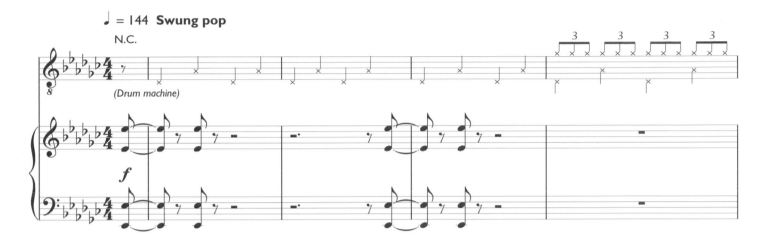

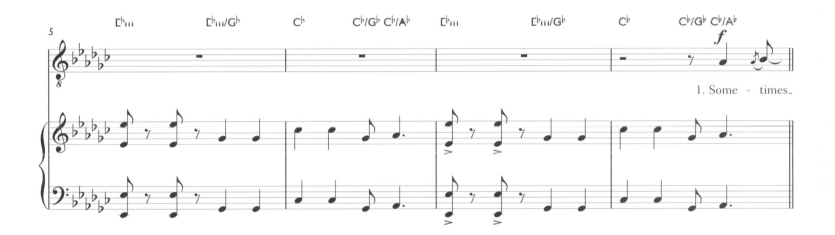

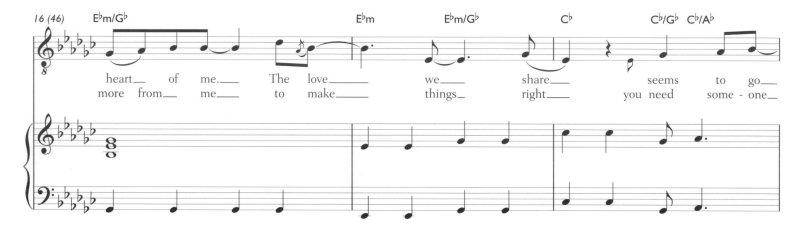

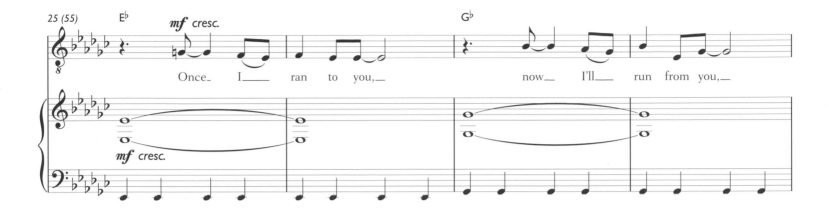

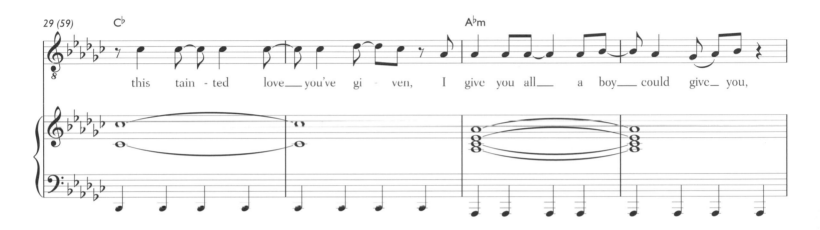

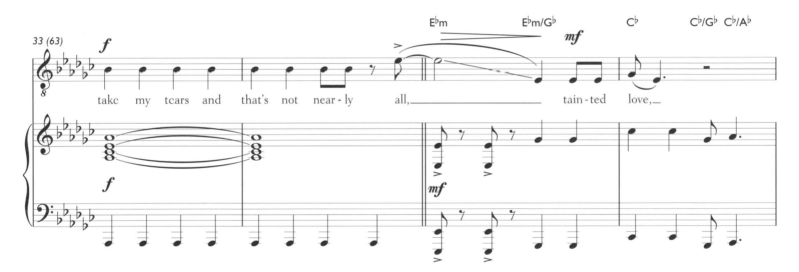

touch me please, I can - not stand___ the way___ you

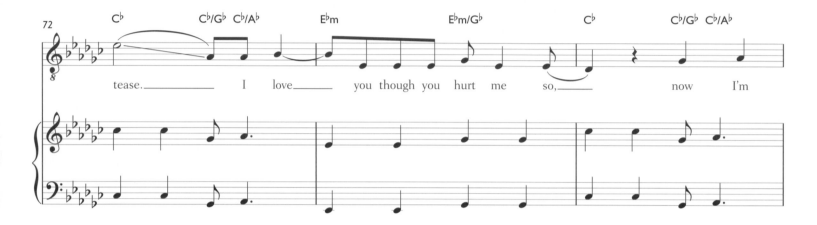

tease.___ I love___ you though you hurt me so,___ now I'm

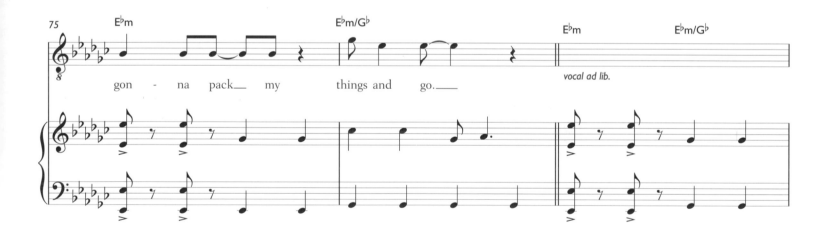

gon - na pack___ my things and go.___

vocal ad lib.

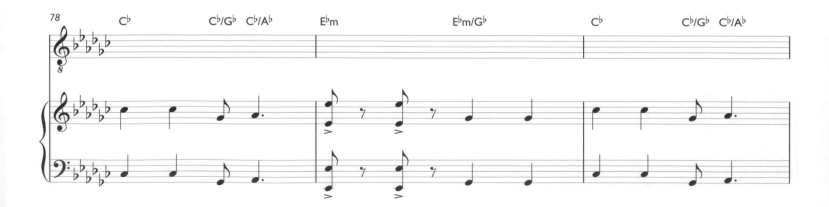

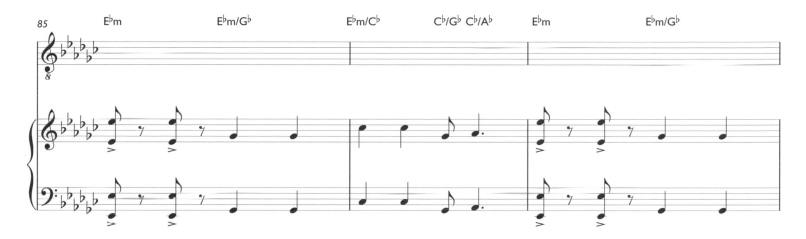

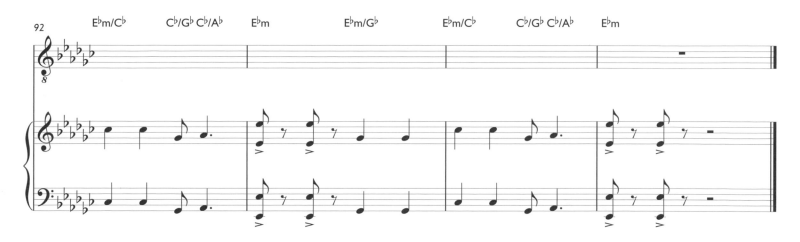

SHE'S OUT OF MY LIFE

In your exam, you will be assessed on the following technical elements:

1 Breath control over longer notes and phrases

This is a slow song with some long notes at the ends of phrases – these require good breath control, particularly as you move up to the high notes. You will need to work out where to breathe: make sure that you can sustain the long notes at the same time as observing the dynamic markings. For example bars 13 and 25 both have a *decrescendo* which needs to be handled with control. The song ends on a *pianissimo* o. Make sure that you hold this note for its full value and use plenty of support to ensure that you maintain the pitch.

2 Tone control across different registers

The wide range of this song means that you will need to move between different registers of the voice. Aim for a smooth transition between registers (for example, between chest voice and head voice), moving smoothly between them without a noticeable break. Be aware of any 'breaks' in your voice – where the tone might become thinner or lacking in intensity.

3 Rhythmic control

Although some of the rhythms in this song are quite complex, you should aim to make them sound natural. Try speaking the lyrics in the more complicated sections, first at a slower speed, articulating the consonants clearly. Aim to make your entries confident and precise. You will need to count carefully to make sure that you come in at exactly the right place each time.

TECHNICAL FOCUS SONGS

demo backing

SHE'S OUT OF MY LIFE

Michael Jackson
Words and Music by Tom Bahler

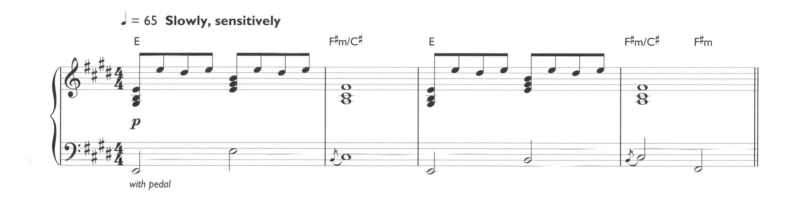

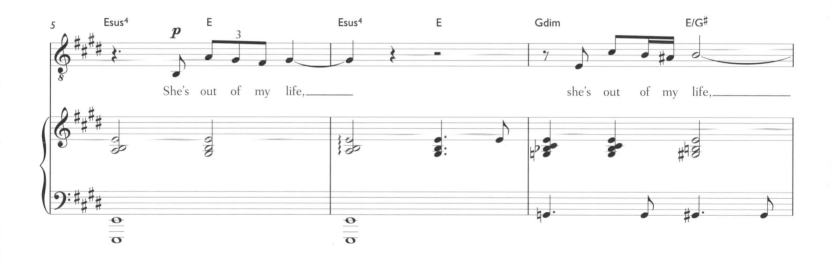

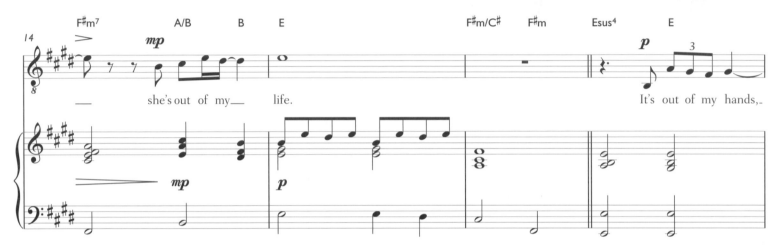

CANNONBALL

Damien Rice

Damien Rice is an Irish singer-songwriter, musician and producer. He began his career during the mid-1990s with the indie rock band Juniper. Disillusioned, Rice left the band following artistic disagreements with the record label. He moved to Tuscany where he became a farmer, also busking and travelling across Europe. On his eventual return to Ireland his second cousin David Arnold, a music producer, was so impressed with Rice's solo work that he bought him a recording studio and invested in him financially.

'Cannonball' is taken from Rice's 2002 debut acoustic album *O* – it met with critical acclaim and has been re-released several times. 'Cannonball' is a folk-influenced love song with enigmatic words: Rice's emotional voice is backed by a gentle acoustic guitar soundscape.

PERFORMANCE · HINTS & TIPS ·

The first part of 'Cannonball' should be sung gently and expressively. This gives you the opportunity to explore the softer, breathier tones of your voice. Much of the song is in the upper range: try adding a tender quality by using a softer tone for some of the higher notes. The song begins softly: the first two verses are *mezzo piano*, but the song grows to *forte* in the final page. Be aware of the subtle changes in dynamics throughout the song and make sure you include them in your performance.

It will help to practise singing some of the wider leaps (e.g. the octaves in bars 7 and 11 and the sixths in bars 29–30 and 37–38) before you learn to sing the whole song. Be clear which note you are jumping from and to. Bar 25 includes a grace note which decorates the melody. Try singing the melody without it at first – this will help you establish the shape of the melody.

'Cannonball' uses syncopated rhythms and in some places the lyrics have been set in an unexpected way. For example, in bars 34–35 the stress has been placed on the second syllable of 'courage'. Be ready for these surprises.

'Love, *it* taught me to *lie*'

ABOUT THE SONGS

I CAN SEE CLEARLY NOW

Johnny Nash

The American singer and songwriter Johnny Nash began singing in his local Baptist church choir in Houston, Texas. He recorded several of his hits in Jamaica, where he worked with Bob Marley (before Marley became a superstar) and his group The Wailers. Marley co-wrote many of the songs on Nash's album *I Can See Clearly Now* (1972).

'I Can See Clearly Now' has an upbeat tempo and optimistic lyrics. It became a big hit and was one of the first songs to bring mainstream acceptance of reggae to the USA. There have been numerous covers of the song. Jimmy Cliff had a big hit with it when he recorded it for the motion picture *Cool Runnings*.

PERFORMANCE · HINTS & TIPS·

This is a happy, optimistic song and you need to float the melody in a light, soulful way to reflect this. The bridge section (starting at bar 40) provides a dramatic contrast to the rest of the song. Make sure you use plenty of support so that you can sing this section loudly and confidently. There is an unexpected twist at the end of this section, where the melody moves down chromatically: practise the tuning of this passage slowly and carefully.

You will need to take a good breath at bar 45 to sustain the phrase 'nothing but blue skies', and again in bar 49 to support the 'Ah' at bar 50. Work on your breathing and practise this section, making sure you don't let the tuning drop as you near the end of your breath.

'It's *gonna* be *a* bright, *sunshiny* day'

WILD HORSES

The Rolling Stones

When they formed as a band in the early 1960s, The Rolling Stones had a keen interest in black American rhythm and blues. Their first albums are mostly covers of R&B songs, but they gradually developed what became the hugely successful Jagger/Richards song-writing partnership – a guitar-driven style combining blues-based hard rock with rhythmic power and pop appeal. Their career spans nearly half a century and they have released more than 100 singles.

'Wild Horses' is taken from the 1971 album *Sticky Fingers*. It is a powerful evocative song and one of the band's few ballads. There have been numerous covers of the song, including versions by Elvis Costello, Neil Young and Deborah Harry.

PERFORMANCE · HINTS & TIPS ·

'Wild Horses' is a slow and expressive song so you will need to make sure you hold the long notes for their full value and take good breaths between the phrases. Make sure that you understand the lyrics so that you can interpret them correctly. Articulate the consonants clearly, especially in the first verse, which should be sung quietly. The second verse is quite loud: make sure this difference in volume is clear and use the shift in dynamics to explore different tone qualities.

Be careful with the pitching and timing of your first entry. Listening for the B in bar 2 of the accompaniment will help. Many of your other entries come between the second and third beats of the bar – practise the timing until you can sing them entirely accurately. The melody moves about quite unexpectedly. You will need to make sure you can pitch all the notes securely as the melody line is often quite independent of the accompaniment.

In the second verse take advantage of the vocal ad lib instruction and ensure you add variation and excitement to your performance.

Look out for the D naturals in bars 23, 27 and 51 and make sure that these are pitched accurately.

'*I* can't *let* you *slide* through *my* hands'

NEUTRON STAR COLLISION

Muse

Muse is made up of three multi-instrumentalists who met when they were at school – Matt Bellamy (vocals, piano and guitar), Christopher Wolstenholme (bass, keyboards and harmonica) and Dominic Howard (drums and electronics). They are well-known for their spectacular live performances. Muse combine a range of different musical styles – including hard rock, electronic, progressive and classical music – to create their own unique sound.

'Neutron Star Collision' was written after Matt Bellamy split with his longtime girlfriend. The lyrics describe his feelings at the beginning of their relationship. The song was used in the soundtrack to the film *The Twilight Saga: Eclipse* and the music video to the single features clips from this film.

PERFORMANCE · HINTS & TIPS ·

This powerful rock song needs to be sung dramatically, with a lot of drive. It starts quite quietly, but you should try to create a feeling of steadily-building energy, following the dynamic markings carefully. Make sure you articulate the consonants clearly: this will help give the song more energy.

The verses need to be sustained and smooth whereas the chorus is loud and dramatic. You should emphasise the contrast between the two. Build the song towards the chorus, where it really needs to come alive. The dynamic is loud so you will need to take some good breaths and make sure that you use plenty of support.

The melody to this song includes several leaps (in, for example, bars 11 and 13). You will need to practise these until you can pitch them securely: the vocals are quite independent of the accompaniment. You could try making some of the trickier phrases into a vocal exercise that you can use to warm up your voice before the song.

'*My* love will be *forever*'

TAINTED LOVE

Soft Cell

Marc Almond and Dave Ball met as art students at Leeds Polytechnic in the late 1970s and went on to form the synth-pop duo Soft Cell in 1980. 'Tainted Love' is included on their album *Non-Stop Erotic Cabaret* (1981) and was a huge international hit in 1981. It is a cover of the northern soul classic first recorded by Gloria Jones in 1965. For their version, Soft Cell slowed down the tempo, changed the key and replaced the guitars and drums with synthesisers and rhythm machines. It has since been covered by numerous groups and artists including Marilyn Manson.

PERFORMANCE · HINTS & TIPS

The melody has some unexpected twists. Look out for the accidentals. There is a double flat (♭♭) in bar 70: this means that you should flatten the note by two semitones. The tune repeatedly drops from G♭ to E♭ on a single syllable throughout the song – for example, on the word 'feel' in bars 9–10. Make sure you move neatly between the two notes – don't slide over them.

There are several grace notes in this song. Try singing the melody without the grace notes at first, so that you can appreciate how the rhythm works. Look closely at the pitch of the grace notes.

In the second verse take advantage of the vocal ad lib instruction and ensure you add variation and excitement to your performance.

'Take *my* tears *and* that's *not* nearly *all*'

SHE'S OUT OF MY LIFE

Michael Jackson

Michael Jackson (1958–2009) was born into a musical family in Indiana, USA. Along with his brothers in The Jackson Five, he was pushed into the music industry at an early age. The band was very successful and achieved the first of several number one hits with their first single. However, most of Michael Jackson's career was as a solo artist. He soon became an international superstar well-known for his expressive singing, his increasingly eccentric behaviour and, not least, his highly accomplished dancing and signature 'moonwalk' dance. His albums with the composer, producer and arranger Quincy Jones set new standards in production.

The emotional ballad 'She's Out Of My Life' is taken from Jackson's first adult solo album *Off The Wall* (1979). On the original recording, it is possible to hear Michael Jackson break down in tears in the final moments of the song.

PERFORMANCE · HINTS & TIPS ·

This song has a wide range – almost two octaves. Always make sure that your voice is thoroughly warmed up before tackling such a big song and use plenty of support on the high notes. It should be sung with a lot of expression, sensitivity and with good breath control. Make sure that you follow the dynamic markings closely.

The song starts with a leap of a seventh – and there are several other wide intervals throughout the song. These add to the emotional impact, as your voice soars up and down. You should practise pitching intervals, learning to recognise the sound of different intervals so that your singing is always accurate and in tune. Look out for the accidentals and make sure you can pitch these notes securely.

'*Now* I've *learned* that *love* needs expression'

SESSION SKILLS

PLAYBACK

For your exam, you can choose either Playback or Improvising (see page 40). If you choose Playback, you will be asked to perform some music you have not seen or heard before.

In the exam, you will be given the song chart and the examiner will play a recording of the music. You will hear several four-bar to eight-bar phrases on the recording: you should sing each of them straight back in turn. There's a rhythm track going throughout, which helps you keep in time. There should not be any gaps in the music.

In the exam you will have two chances to perform with the recording:
- First time – for practice
- Second time – for assessment

You should listen to the audio, copying what you hear; you can also read the music. Here are some practice song charts which are also on the CD in this book. The music is printed without text and may be sung to any vowel (with or without consonant) or to sol-fa. Some of the examples may include accents so you may need to use consonants or scat words for these to make them really obvious.

Don't forget that the Playback test can include requirements which may not be shown in these examples, including those from earlier grades. Check the parameters at www.trinityrock.com to prepare for everything which might come up in your exam.

'I really *like* the *way* music *looks* on *paper.* It *looks* like *art* to *me*'

Steve Vai

Practice playback 1

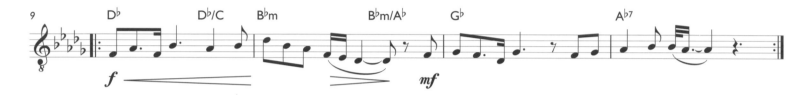

Practice playback 2

TRACK 14

SESSION SKILLS
IMPROVING

For your exam, you can choose either Playback (see page 37), or Improvising. If you choose to improvise, you will be asked to improvise over a backing track that you haven't heard before in a specified style.

In the exam, you will be given a song chart and the examiner will play a recording of the backing track. The backing track consists of a passage of music played on a loop. You should improvise a melody line over the backing track.

In the exam you will have two chances to perform with the recording:
- First time – for practice
- Second time – for assessment

Here are some improvising charts for practice which are also on the CD in this book. The music is printed without text and may be sung to any vowel (with or without consonant) or to sol-fa.

Don't forget that the Improvising test can include requirements which may not be shown in these examples, including those from earlier grades. Check the parameters at www.trinityrock.com to prepare for everything which might come up in your exam.

Practice improvisation 1

TRACK 15

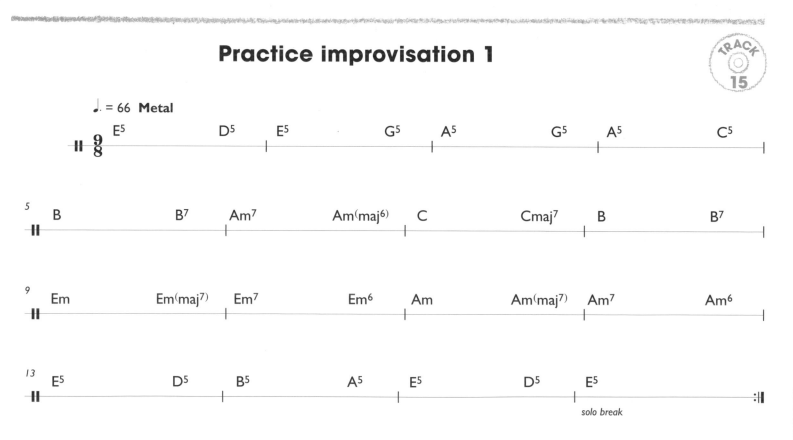

Practice improvisation 2

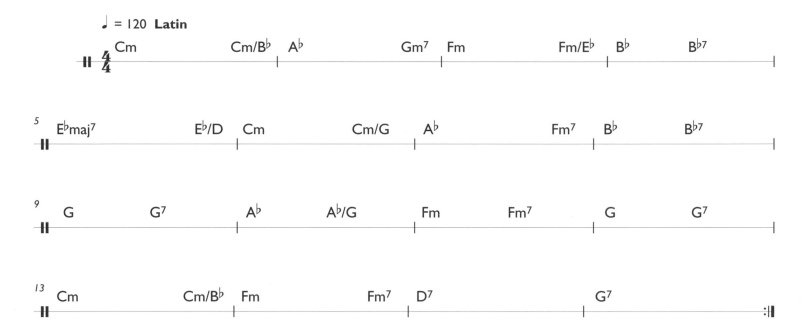

♩ = 120 **Latin**

𝄃 4/4 | Cm | Cm/B♭ A♭ | Gm⁷ Fm | Fm/E♭ B♭ B♭⁷ |

⁵ 𝄃 E♭maj⁷ | E♭/D Cm | Cm/G A♭ | Fm⁷ B♭ B♭⁷ |

⁹ 𝄃 G G⁷ | A♭ A♭/G | Fm Fm⁷ | G G⁷ |

¹³ 𝄃 Cm | Cm/B♭ Fm | Fm⁷ D⁷ | G⁷ 𝄂

'Relax.
Enjoy yourself.
Play *a lot.*'

Joe Satriani

CHOOSING A SONG FOR YOUR EXAM

There are lots of options to help you choose your three songs for the exam. For Songs 1 and 2, you can choose a song which is:

- from this book
- from www.trinityrock.com

Or for Song 2 you can choose a song which is:

- sheet music from a printed or online source.
- your own arrangement of a song or a song you have written yourself.

You can perform the song unaccompanied or with a backing track (minus the solo voice). If you like, you can create a backing track yourself (or with friends). For Grade 6, the song should last between two-and-a-half and four minutes, and the level of difficulty should be similar to your other songs. When choosing a song, think about:

- Does it work for my voice?
- Are there any technical elements that are too difficult for me? (If so, perhaps save it for when you do the next grade.)
- Do I enjoy singing it?
- Does it work with my other songs to create a good set-list?

See www.trinityrock.com for further information and advice on choosing your own song.

SHEET MUSIC

For your exam, you must always bring an original copy of the book or a download sheets with email certificate / proof of purchase for each song you perform in the exam. If you choose to write your own song you must provide the examiner with a copy of your music.

Your music can be:

- a lead sheet with lyrics, chords and melody line
- a chord chart with lyrics
- a full score using conventional staff notation

The title of the song and your name should be on the sheet music.

IMPROVISING IN SONGS

Improvising is an exciting and creative way to make the music your own. Improvisation might include singing your own melody line, ad-libbing around a given tune or making up an accompaniment. Rock and pop music often includes opportunities for musicians to improvise during a song – it is a great way to display your instrumental/vocal skills and musical abilities.

Make sure you know the song well and feel comfortable and confident with the rhythms, chord progressions and the general groove that underpins the music. Once you're familiar with it, the best way to learn how to improvise is to do it!

Some useful starting points might be:

- Identify just a few notes that sound good over the chord progressions, and experiment with these first.
- Add more notes as your musical ideas start to develop – improvising is often most effective when a simple idea is repeated, varied and extended.
- You don't need to fill every gap! Silence can be an important – and very effective – part of your improvisation.
- The more you improvise – and experiment – the better you will become, until your improvisations seem effortless.

It's important to be aware of the tonality of the song and to recognise different scales and modes that are appropriate to use. Start by familiarising yourself with:

- the minor pentatonic scale
- the blues scale
- the Dorian mode
- major and minor scales

You might find it useful to listen to some original versions of different rock and pop songs. Have a go at learning the vocal solos in these versions – this will help you to develop an understanding of how other musicians develop musical material.

HELP PAGES

PERFORMING

Being well prepared is the secret of a good performance. The more you practise, the better you will perform.

Top Ten Practice Tips

1 Develop a regular practice routine. Try to set aside a certain amount of time every day.

2 Choose specific things to practise each week.

3 Set goals for each practice session and continually review your progress.

4 Sing a wide variety of songs – not just your favourites over and over again – to increase your skill and adaptability.

5 Identify the parts of the songs you find difficult and give them special attention.

6 Practise those techniques that you struggle with as well as those you find easier.

7 Don't reinforce mistakes by repeating them over and over again.

8 Include warm-ups and technical exercises in your practice sessions as well as songs.

9 Use a metronome.

10 Record yourself on audio or video. Listen to your older recordings to see how much you have improved.

Try to memorise the music – aim to sound free and natural and put your own stamp on the songs.

PERFORMING

BEFORE YOUR PERFORMANCE

- Watch and listen to others perform. Go to live performances and watch some videos online. Think about the aspects of performances you particularly like and try them out.
- Practise singing in front of an audience and communicate with them.
- Learn some relaxation and breathing exercises.
- Be positive about your performance. Think about how good your performance will be.
- Know your music.

ON THE DAY OF YOUR PERFORMANCE

- Wear something comfortable.
- Try some physical exercises.
- Warm up.
- Do some relaxation and breathing exercises.

THE PERFORMANCE

Your audience may be large or small – and in an exam may only be one person – but it is important to give a sense of performance no matter how many people are present.

- Walk into the room confidently.
- Keep your head up, so you can look at your audience and acknowledge them.
- Focus on the music.
- Look confident and keep going, no matter what happens.
- Engage with your audience.
- Enjoy yourself.

YOUR PAGE

NOTES

PERFORMING WITH BACKING TRACKS

The CD contains demos and backing tracks of all the songs in the book. The additional songs at www.trinityrock.com also come with demos and backing tracks.

- In your exam, you can perform with the backing track, or create your own.
- The backing tracks begin with a click track, which sets the tempo and helps you start accurately.
- Be careful to balance the volume of the backing track against your voice.
- Listen carefully to the backing track to ensure you are singing in time.

If you are creating your own backing track, here are some further tips:
- Make sure the sound quality is of a good standard.
- Think carefully about the instruments/sounds you are putting on the backing track.
- Avoid copying what you are singing on the backing track – it should support not duplicate.
- Do you need to include a click track at the beginning?

COPYRIGHT IN A SONG

If you are a singer or songwriter it is important to know about copyright. When someone writes a song or creates an arrangement they own the copyright (sometimes called 'the rights') to that version. The copyright means that other people cannot copy it, sell it, perform it in a concert, make it available online or record it without the owner's permission or the appropriate licence. When you write a song you automatically own the copyright to it, which means that other people cannot copy your work. But just as importantly, you cannot copy other people's work, or perform it in public without their permission or the appropriate licence.

Points to remember
- You can create a cover version of a song for an exam or other non-public performance.
- You cannot record your cover version and make your recording available to others (by copying it or uploading it to a website) without the appropriate licence.
- You own the copyright of your own original song, which means that no one is allowed to copy it.
- You cannot copy someone else's song without their permission or the appropriate licence.
- If you would like to use somebody else's words in your own song you must check if they are in copyright and, if so, we recommend you confirm with the author that they are happy for the words to be used as lyrics.
- Materials protected by copyright can normally be used as lyrics in our examinations as these are private performances under copyright law. The examiner may ask you the name of the original author in the exam.
- When you present your own song to the examiner, make sure you include the title, the names of any writers and the source of your lyrics.

ROCK & POP EXAMS

ALSO AVAILABLE

Trinity College London Rock & Pop examinations 2012-2017 are also available for:

Bass Initial
ISBN: 978-0-85736-227-8

Bass Grade 1
ISBN: 978-0-85736-228-5

Bass Grade 2
ISBN: 978-0-85736-229-2

Bass Grade 3
ISBN: 978-0-85736-230-8

Bass Grade 4
ISBN: 978-0-85736-231-5

Bass Grade 5
ISBN: 978-0-85736-232-2

Bass Grade 6
ISBN: 978-0-85736-233-9

Bass Grade 7
ISBN: 978-0-85736-234-6

Bass Grade 8
ISBN: 978-0-85736-235-3

Drums Initial
ISBN: 978-0-85736-245-2

Drums Grade 1
ISBN: 978-0-85736-246-9

Drums Grade 2
ISBN: 978-0-85736-247-6

Drums Grade 3
ISBN: 978-0-85736-248-3

Drums Grade 4
ISBN: 978-0-85736-249-0

Drums Grade 5
ISBN: 978-0-85736-250-6

Drums Grade 6
ISBN: 978-0-85736-251-3

Drums Grade 7
ISBN: 978-0-85736-252-0

Drums Grade 8
ISBN: 978-0-85736-253-7

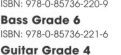

Guitar Initial
ISBN: 978-0-85736-218-6

Guitar Grade 1
ISBN: 978-0-85736-219-3

Guitar Grade 2
ISBN: 978-0-85736-220-9

Bass Grade 6
ISBN: 978-0-85736-221-6

Guitar Grade 4
ISBN: 978-0-85736-222-3

Guitar Grade 5
ISBN: 978-0-85736-223-0

Guitar Grade 6
ISBN: 978-0-85736-224-7

Guitar Grade 7
ISBN: 978-0-85736-225-4

Guitar Grade 8
ISBN: 978-0-85736-226-1

Keyboards Initial
ISBN: 978-0-85736-236-0

Keyboards Grade 1
ISBN: 978-0-85736-237-7

Keyboards Grade 2
ISBN: 978-0-85736-238-4

Keyboards Grade 3
ISBN: 978-0-85736-239-1

Keyboards Grade 4
ISBN: 978-0-85736-240-7

Keyboards Grade 5
ISBN: 978-0-85736-241-4

Keyboards Grade 6
ISBN: 978-0-85736-242-1

Keyboards Grade 7
ISBN: 978-0-85736-243-8

Keyboards Grade 8
ISBN: 978-0-85736-244-5

Vocals Initial
ISBN: 978-0-85736-254-4

Vocals Grade 1
ISBN: 978-0-85736-255-1

Vocals Grade 2
ISBN: 978-0-85736-256-8

Vocals Grade 3
ISBN: 978-0-85736-257-5

Vocals Grade 4
ISBN: 978-0-85736-258-2

Vocals Grade 5
ISBN: 978-0-85736-259-9

Vocals Grade 6 (female voice)
ISBN: 978-0-85736-263-6

Vocals Grade 6 (male voice)
ISBN: 978-0-85736-260-5

Vocals Grade 7 (female voice)
ISBN: 978-0-85736-264-3

Vocals Grade 7 (male voice)
ISBN: 978-0-85736-261-2

Vocals Grade 8 (female voice)
ISBN: 978-0-85736-265-0

Vocals Grade 8 (male voice)
ISBN: 978-0-85736-262-9